Tips & Quotes

My Sketches & Doodles

My Notes, lists & Doodles

Compiled by Kitty Edwards

Created by Flame Tree Studio

Publisher and Creative Director: Nick Wells
Senior Project Editor: Catherine Taylor
Art Director and Layout Design: Mike Spender

Special thanks to: Emma Scigliano

FLAME TREE PUBLISHING
6 Melbray Mews
Fulham, London SW6 3NS
United Kingdom

www.flametreepublishing.com

First published 2016

16 18 20 19 17
1 3 5 7 9 10 8 6 4 2

Images courtesy of Sonia Leong, Shutterstock.com and the following contributors:
mashabr, Artex67, Valenty, Lyudmyla Kharlamova, bioraven, balabolka, topform, PavloArt Studio,
SS1001, Christos Georghiou, Bimbim, Katja Gerasimova, baldyrgan, NikolayN, VAlex, Lolla Lenn,
ArtMari, Aluna1, Danussa, Yoko Design, Yucatana, Mike Demidov, isaxar, Phant, R_lion_O, mis-Tery,
Janna Mudrak, Mirumur, NailGM, Katja Gerasimova, Littlegirl, L. Kramer, MaKars, Vecster,
karakotsya, Torikka Zhurova, oksanka007, Palomita, tanvetka, Nikolaeva, Ohn Mar, Havroshechka,
Nikolaeva, bioraven, Chiociolla, insima, Vracovska, Catherine Glazkova, L. Kramer, Maria Bo,
IRINA RAIDO, Vorobiew Aleksey, Fernando Cortes, Involved Channel, psynovec.

ISBN 978-1-78664-054-3

Printed in China

Contents

Finish This 4

Try This 44

Inspiration 92

Art Calendar 150

My Sketches & Clippings 156

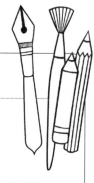

The Wheel

Fill in the sections on the wheel with paint or pencil, thinking about primary and secondary hues, tints, tones and shades.

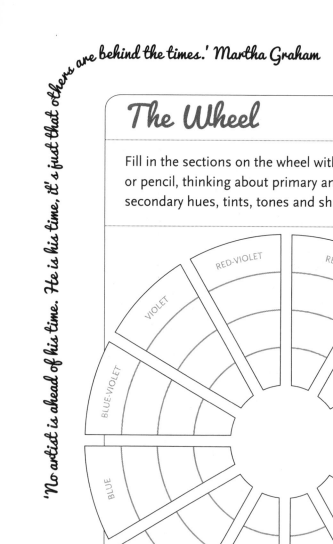

RED-VIOLET

RED

VIOLET

RED-ORANGE

BLUE-VIOLET

ORANGE

BLUE

YELLOW-ORANGE

BLUE-GREEN

YELLOW

GREEN

YELLOW-GREEN

Tip: Always add dark paint to light paint when mixing, do so slowly with caution until the desired effect is reached.

'I will be an artist or nothing!' Eugene O'Neill

Shade This

Complete the images by shading in the outlines.

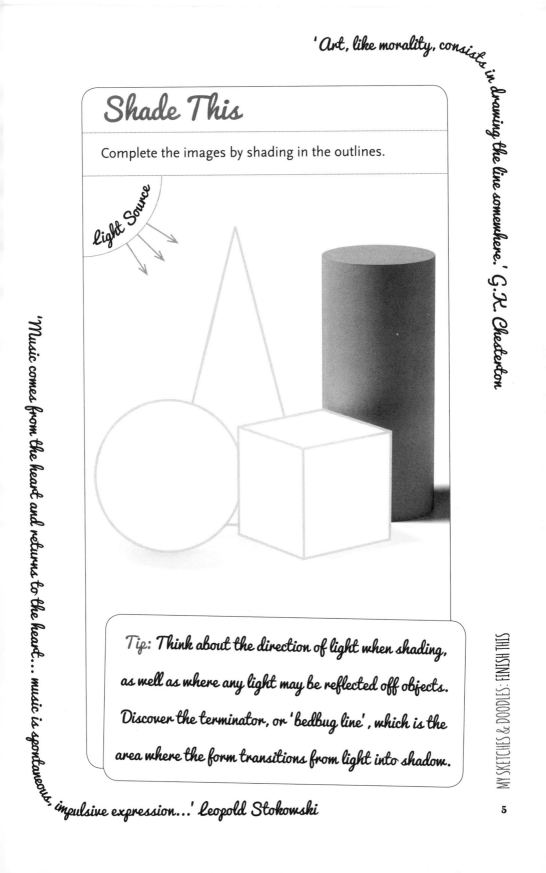

Light Source

Tip: Think about the direction of light when shading, as well as where any light may be reflected off objects. Discover the terminator, or 'bedbug line', which is the area where the form transitions from light into shadow.

'Music comes from the heart and returns to the heart… music is spontaneous, impulsive expression…' Leopold Stokowski

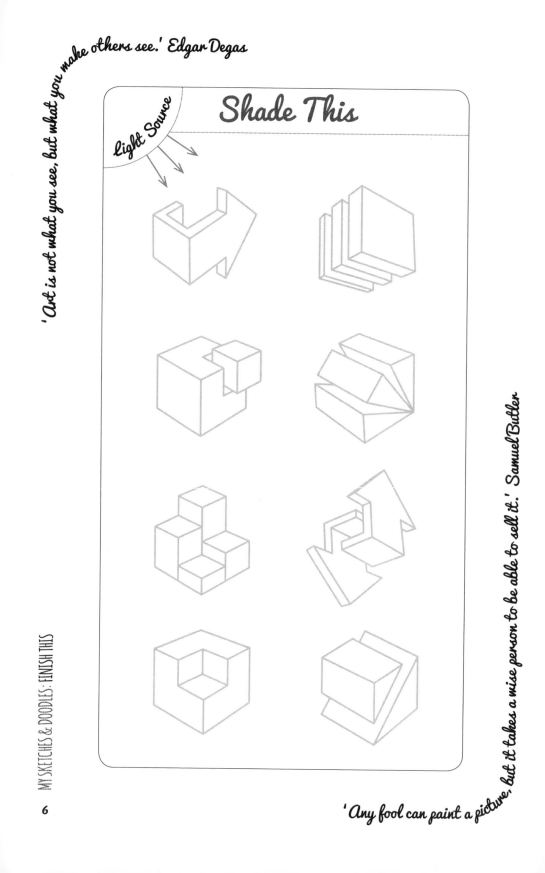

'Art is not what you see, but what you make others see.' Edgar Degas

Shade This

Light Source

'Any fool can paint a picture, but it takes a wise person to be able to sell it.' Samuel Butler

Shade This

Light Source

'Art is literacy of the heart.' Elliot Eisner

Picture This

Use the backgrounds provided here as inspiration
to add your foregrounds and/or subjects.
This first one has an example already to get you started.

'Creativity takes courage.' Henri Matisse

Picture This

'Art washes away from the soul the dust of everyday life.' Pablo Picasso

Picture This

'Those who do not want to imitate anything, produce nothing.' Salvador Dalí

Picture This

'To create one's own world takes courage.' Georgia O'Keeffe

Picture This

'If you hear a voice within you say you cannot paint, then by all means paint

'Painting is the silence of thought and the music of sight.' Orhan Pamuk, "My Name is Red"

Picture This

'Every portrait that is painted with feeling is a portrait of the artist, not of the sitter.' Oscar Wilde, "The Picture of Dorian Gray"

Picture This

Picture This

'It is not bright colours but good drawing that makes figures beautiful.' Titian

Picture This

'I find him in the curves of certain lines, in the loveliness and subtleties of certain colours.' Oscar Wilde, "The Picture of Dorian Gray"

Picture This

'All you need to paint is a few tools, a little instruction, and a vision in your mind.' Bob Ross

'A painting requires a little mystery, some vagueness, and some fantasy. When you always make your meaning perfectly plain you end up boring people.' Edgar Degas

Picture This

'I say that good painters imitated nature; but that bad ones vomited it.' Miguel de Cervantes

Picture This

Complete This

Complete the drawing based
on the partial image.

MY SKETCHES & DOODLES · FINISH THIS

'The object of art is not to reproduce reality, but to create a reality

'It is important to express oneself...provided the feelings are real and are taken from you own experience.' Berthe Morisot

Complete This

'In art, the hand can never execute anything higher than the heart can imagine.' Ralph Waldo Emerson

Complete This

'Whether you succeed or not is irrelevant, there is no such thing. Making your un

'Every good painter paints what he is.' Jackson Pollock

Complete This

'Art must be an expression of love or it is nothing.' Marc Chagall

Complete This

Complete This

'Life obliges me to do something, so I paint.' René Magritte

Complete This

'A guilty conscience needs to confess. A work of art is a confession.' Albert Camus

Complete This

Complete This

'Many are willing to suffer for their art. Few are willing to learn to draw.' Simon Munnery, "Attention Scum"

Complete This

Complete This

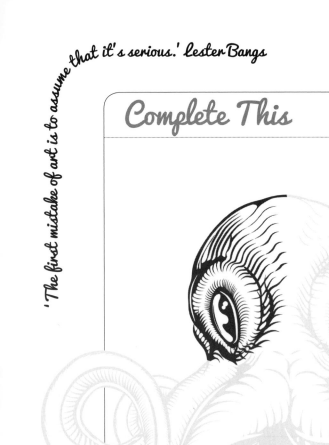

'Color is only beautiful when it means something.' Robert Henri

Complete This

'The picture will have charm when each colour is very unlike the one next to it.' Leon Battista Alberti

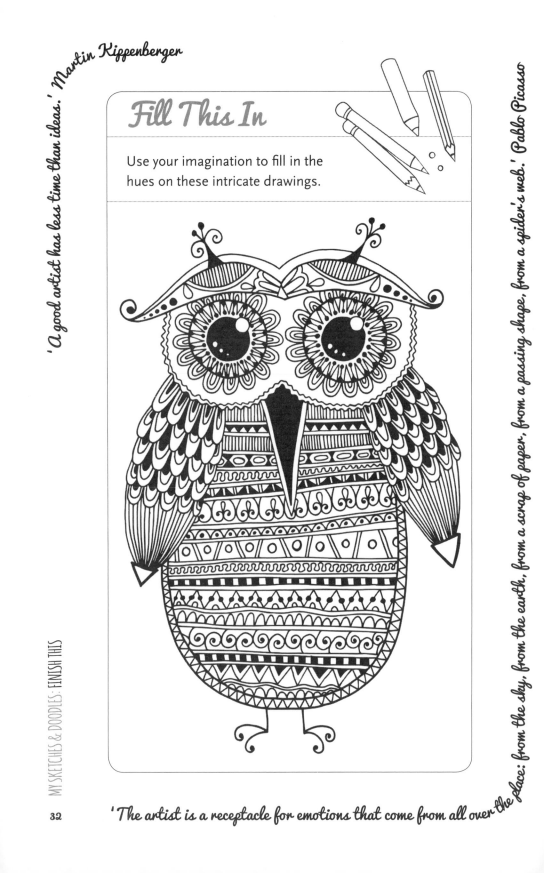

'A good artist has less time than ideas.' Martin Kippenberger

Fill This In

Use your imagination to fill in the hues on these intricate drawings.

'The artist is a receptacle for emotions that come from all over the place: from the sky, from the earth, from a scrap of paper, from a passing shape, from a spider's web.' Pablo Picasso

Fill This In

"Drawing is the root that keeps painting alive.' Connie Sharp

Fill This In

'The longer you look at an object, the more abstract it becomes, and, ironically, the more real.' Lucian Freud

Fill This In

"Don't think about making art, just get it done. Let everyone else decide if it's good or bad, whether they love it or hate it. While they are deciding, make even more art.' Andy Warhol

Fill This In

'Poor is the pupil who does not surpass his master.' Leonardo da Vinci

Fill This In

'Nature is not only all that is visible to the eye... it also includes the inner pictures of the soul.' Edvard Munch

Fill This In

'The holy grail is to spend less time making the picture than it takes people to look at it.' Banksy

Fill This In

'I don't say everything, but I paint everything.' Pablo Picasso

Fill This In

'Weirdism is definitely the cornerstone of many an artist's career.' E.A. Bucchianeri, "Brushstrokes of a Gadfly"

Fill This In

' Art is communication.' Madeleine L'Engle

'Color is like cooking. The cook puts in more or less salt, that's the difference!' Josef Albers

Fill This In

'Colors speak all languages.' Joseph Addison

Fill This In

'And, of course, I began drawing so much — wild, undisciplined pencil drawings and watercolors of knights battling and such.' Andrew Wyeth

Try Drawing Still Life

Arrange selections of objects and practice
drawing them from different angles,
in different settings and in different styles.

Tip: *If you don't have time to draw a whole still life
in one sitting, put it where it can be left untouched.
That way the position of the objects doesn't change
and the perspective on the piece remains the same.*

'For me, painting is a way to forget life. It is a cry in the night, a strangled laugh.' Georges Rouault

Try Drawing Still Life

First try copying the examples opposite, and on the following pages. Then try your own.

Try Drawing Still Life

Try Drawing Still Life

'One can have no smaller or greater mastery than mastery of oneself.' Leonardo da Vinci

'An artist never really finishes his work; he merely abandons it.' Paul Valéry

MY SKETCHES & DOODLES : STILL ART

Try Drawing Still Life

'The aim of art is to represent not the outward appearance of things, but their inward significance.' Aristotle

Try Drawing Still Life

'To send light into the darkness of men's hearts – such is the duty of the artist.' Schumann

Try Drawing Still Life

Now try your own

Try Drawing Still Life

'Art is not about thinking something up. It is the opposite getting something down.' Julia Cameron

'...I do not want art for a few; any more than education for a few; or freedom for a few...' William Morris

Try Drawing Still Life

Now try your own

'If you don't want a generation of robots, fund the arts!' Cath Crowley, "Graffiti Moon"

Try Drawing Still Life

'I have always tended to start with drawings. It's a very ancient, very normal way of doing it...' Deon Venter

Try Drawing Still Life

Now try your own

'Do not fail, as you go on, to draw something every day, for no matter how little it is, it will be well worth while, and it will do you a world of good.' Cennino Cennini

Try Drawing Still Life

Try Figure Drawing

Ideally find someone who is happy to
sit/stand for you for a short sketch,
or try drawing human forms from memory.

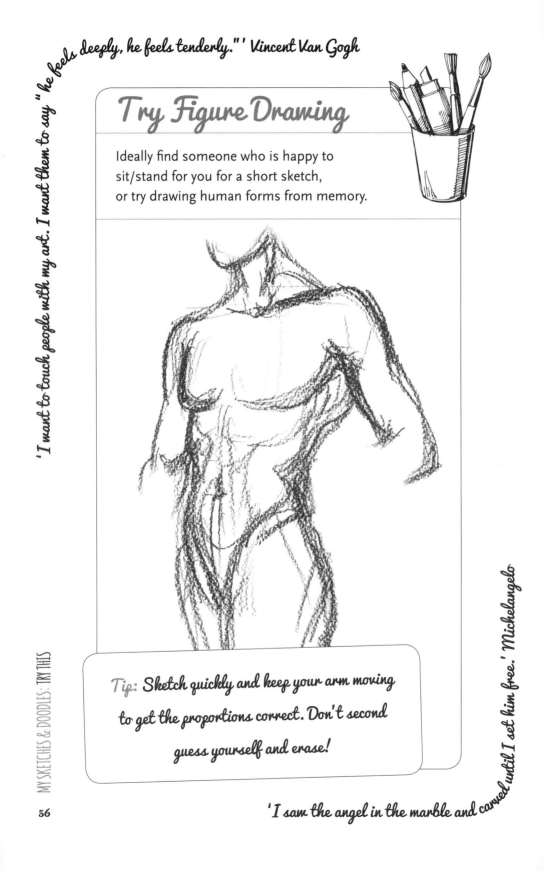

Tip: Sketch quickly and keep your arm moving
to get the proportions correct. Don't second
guess yourself and erase!

'I want to touch people with my art. I want them to say

'I saw the angel in the marble and carved until I set him free.' Michelangelo

Try Figure Drawing

First try copying the examples opposite, and on the following pages. Then try your own.

Try Figure Drawing

'Creativity is allowing yourself to make mistakes. Art is knowing

'Painting is easy when you don't know how, but very difficult when you do.' Edgar Degas

Try Figure Drawing

Try Figure Drawing

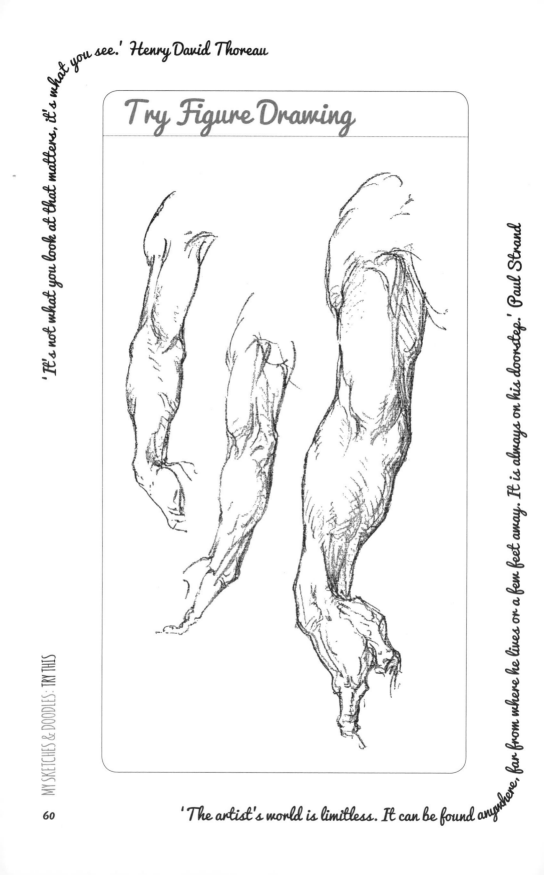

'The artist's world is limitless. It can be found anywhere, far from where he lives or a few feet away. It is always on his doorstep.' Paul Strand

Try Figure Drawing

'Without tradition, art is a flock of sheep without a shepherd. Without innovation, it is a corpse.' Winston Churchill

Try Figure Drawing

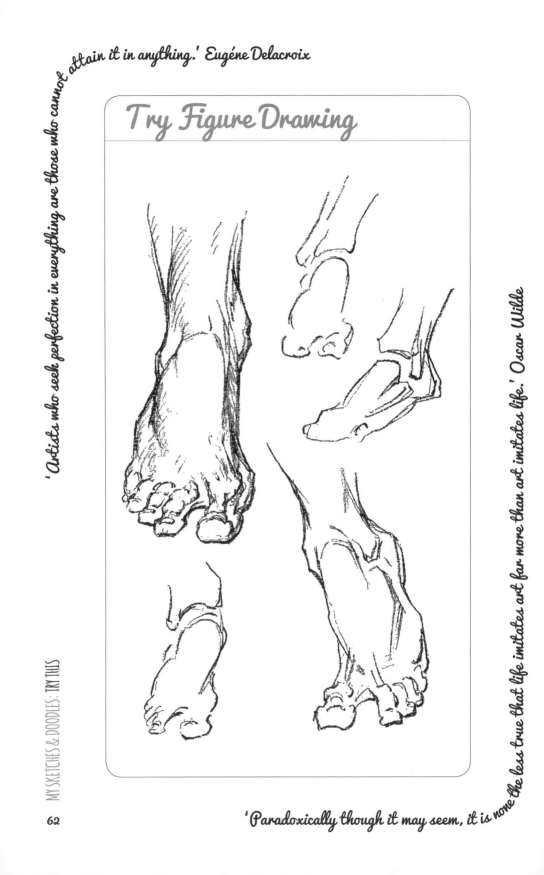

Try Figure Drawing

Try Figure Drawing

Now try
your own

'Now art should never try to be popular. The public should try to make itself artistic.' Oscar Wilde

Try Figure Drawing

Try Figure Drawing

Now try
your own

'Art is, after all, only a trace like a footprint which shows that one has walked bravely and in great happiness.' Robert Henri

Try Figure Drawing

'I am an artist you know ... it is my right to be odd.' E.A. Bucchianeri, "Brushstrokes of a Gadfly"

Try Drawing Movement

Site yourself in a busy location such as a shopping mall, or at a racetrack, and try to capture the way figures move.

Tip: Roughly draw a series of movement sketches one on top of the other over a period of time, to get a sense of how the object moves.

'Drawing is the foundation of the painting to familiarize yourself with the subject and to work out problems of perspective and proportion.' Michael Nevin

Try Drawing Movement

First try copying the examples opposite, and on the following pages. Then try your own.

Try Drawing Movement

'To practice any art, no matter how well or badly, is a way to make your soul grow. So do it.' Kurt Vonnegut

Try Drawing Movement

Try Drawing Movement

'Everything has its beauty, but not everyone sees it.' Andy Warhol

Try Drawing Movement

Try Drawing Movement

Now try
your own

'Art does not exist only to entertain, but also to challenge one to think, to provoke, even to disturb,

Try Drawing Movement

'I paint my own reality. The only thing I know is that I paint because I need to, and I paint whatever passes through my head without any other consideration.' Frida Kahlo

Try Drawing Movement

Now try your own

'People say graffiti is ugly, irresponsible and childish... but that's only if it's done properly.' Banksy, " Wall and Piece"

Try Drawing Movement

Try Drawing Movement

Now try
your own

'Artists are people driven by the tension between the desire to communicate and the desire to hide.' D.W. Winnicott

'It is through art, and through art only, that we can realise our perfection.' Oscar Wilde

Try Drawing Movement

'All worthy work is open to interpretations the author did not intend. Art isn't your pet – it's your kid. It grows up and talks back to you.' Joss Whedon

Try Drawing Landscapes

Ideally choose an expansive view to sketch from life, such as out of your bedroom window, on holiday or at a park. You may wish to turn the book on its side!

Tips: For traditionally pleasing pictures, use the Rule of Thirds, whereby the picture grid is divided into equal thirds, vertically and horizontally, then subjects are placed along the lines, at their intersection points or across all three sections, while the horizon is along the top or bottom line.

'A painting is never finished – it simply stops in interesting places.' Paul Gardner

Try Drawing Landscapes

First try copying the examples opposite, and on the following pages. Then try your own.

Try Drawing Landscapes

'There is nothing more riveting than drawing and painting. Through them we face our individual character and the individual character of the viewer.' Laura Higgins Palmer

Try Drawing Landscapes

'You come to nature with all her theories, and she knocks them all flat.' Pierre Auguste Renoir

Try Drawing Landscapes

'... the reproduction of what the senses perceive in nature, seen through the veil of the soul.' Paul Cézanne

'If I were called upon to define briefly the word Art, I should call it

Try Drawing Landscapes

'I invent nothing, I rediscover.' Auguste Rodin

Try Drawing Landscapes

Now try your own

'The important thing is to keep on drawing when you start to paint. Never graduate from drawing.' John Sloan

Try Drawing Landscapes

'A good drawing has immense vitality because it is explanatory. In a good drawing even its faults have become virtues.' John Sloan

Try Drawing Landscapes

Now try
your own

'You can eliminate color and still have a painting that works, but you must have drawing, value and design.' Matt Smith

Try Drawing Landscapes

'To be an artist means never to avert one's eyes.' Akira Kurosawa

'If you're going to draw a comic strip every day, you're going to have to draw on every experience in your life.' Charles Schulz

Try Drawing Landscapes

Now try your own

'Painting: The art of protecting flat surfaces from the weather and exposing

'Drawing is the poet's written line, set down to see if there be a story worth telling, a truth worth revealing.' Irving Stone

Try Drawing Landscapes

"Drawing is an act of commitment and of laying bare one's soul, yet perhaps should be kept as routine as a simple daily walk in fresh air.' Karen Gillis Taylor

Artworks I love

Name of piece:

Artist:

Style/Movement:

Year painted:

Medium:

Where:

Description:

Influences:

Comments:

'We may be wrong, but we take leap after leap in the dark.' Agnes de Mille

'The artist never entirely knows. We guess.

Artworks I love

Name of piece:

Artist:

Style/Movement:

Year painted:

Medium:

Where:

Description:

Influences:

Comments:

Artworks I love

Name of piece:

Artist:

Style/Movement:

Year painted:

Medium:

Where:

Description:

Influences:

Comments:

'When I say artist I mean the one who is building things & some with a brush,

'The artist is always beginning. Any work of art which is not a beginning, an invention, a discovery is of little worth.' Ezra Pound

Artworks I love

Name of piece:

Artist:

Style/Movement:

Year painted:

Medium:

Where:

Description:

Influences:

Comments:

'The unfed mind devours itself.' Gore Vidal

Artworks I love

Name of piece:

Artist:

Style/Movement:

Year painted:

Medium:

Where:

Description:

Influences:

Comments:

'Life is the art of drawing without an eraser.' John W. Gardner.

Artworks I love

Name of piece:

Artist:

Style/Movement:

Year painted:

Medium:

Where:

Description:

Influences:

Comments:

Artworks I love

Name of piece:

Artist:

Style/Movement:

Year painted:

Medium:

Where:

Description:

Influences:

Comments:

MY SKETCHES & DOODLES: INSPIRATION

'One must keep right on drawing; draw with your eyes when you cannot draw with a pencil.' Jean-Auguste-Dominique Ingres

Artworks I love

Name of piece:

Artist:

Style/Movement:

Year painted:

Medium:

Where:

Description:

Influences:

Comments:

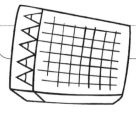

Artworks I love

Name of piece:

Artist:

Style/Movement:

Year painted:

Medium:

Where:

Description:

Influences:

Comments:

'Drawing is a way of reserving a place for color in advance.' Andre L'Hote

'You can only learn to paint by drawing.'

Artworks I love

Name of piece:

Artist:

Style/Movement:

Year painted:

Medium:

Where:

Description:

Influences:

Comments:

Artworks I love

Name of piece:

Artist:

Style/Movement:

Year painted:

Medium:

Where:

Description:

Influences:

Comments:

'I shun drawing which is too easily formulated. It does not seem fertilized enough to produce consequences, and a drawing should be a provider of consequences.' Rico Lebrun

Artworks I love

Name of piece:

Artist:

Style/Movement:

Year painted:

Medium:

Where:

Description:

Influences:

Comments:

' Seemingly the most easy of crafts, drawing is the one which reveals most tellingly our incapacity to sustain true vision and our acquiescence to the ready-made.' Rico Lebrun

Galleries, Shows & Exhibitions

Date:

Place:

Show title:

Artist(s) featured:

Comments:

'A drawing is always dragged down to the level of its caption.'

James Thurber

'Art doesn't have to be pretty. It has to be meaningful.' Duane Hanson

Galleries, Shows & Exhibitions

Date:

Place:

Show title:

Artist (s) featured:

Comments:

'To draw, you must close your eyes and sing.' Pablo Picasso

MY SKETCHES & DOODLES : INSPIRATION

105

Galleries, Shows & Exhibitions

Date:

Place:

Show title:

Artist (s) featured:

Comments:

'Every good painting must be based on a good drawing. Drawing is like the bones to the human body.' Diana Kan

Galleries, Shows & Exhibitions

Date:

Place:

Show title:

Artist (s) featured:

Comments:

'Art is not a thing, it is a way.' Elbert Hubbard

MY SKETCHES & DOODLES : INSPIRATION

107

'I am interested in art as a means of living a life; not as a means of making a living.' Robert Henri

Galleries, Shows & Exhibitions

Date:

Place:

Show title:

Artist (s) featured:

Comments:

'If one draws the subject precisely, only then can the freedom of brushstroke be achieved.' Gayle Lee

Galleries, Shows & Exhibitions

Date:

Place:

Show title:

Artist (s) featured:

Comments:

'Drawing offers a unique record of an encounter with a culture, of experience transformed from fleeting moment to lasting resonance.' Deane G. Keller

MY SKETCHES & DOODLES : INSPIRATION

109

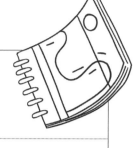

Galleries, Shows & Exhibitions

Date:

Place:

Show title:

Artist (s) featured:

Comments:

'When I can't paint, I can draw, and this simple but very powerful tool gets me back to the very door of creativity.' Pat Corbin Henson

Galleries, Shows & Exhibitions

Date:

Place:

Show title:

Artist (s) featured:

Comments:

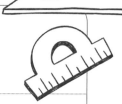

Galleries, Shows & Exhibitions

Date:

Place:

Show title:

Artist (s) featured:

Comments:

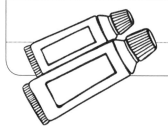

'Drawing is rather like playing chess: your mind races ahead of the moves that you eventually make.' David Hockney

Galleries, Shows & Exhibitions

Date:

Place:

Show title:

Artist (s) featured:

Comments:

ART

Galleries, Shows & Exhibitions

Date:

Place:

Show title:

Artist (s) featured:

Comments:

Galleries, Shows & Exhibitions

Date:

Place:

Show title:

Artist(s) featured:

Comments:

Artists I love

Name:

Style:

Years active:

Movement:

Media:

Influences:

Comments:

'I draw like other people bite their nails.'
Pablo Picasso

'You can never do too much drawing.' Tintoretto

Artists I love

Name:

Style:

Years active:

Movement:

Media:

Influences:

Comments:

'She never looked nice. She looked like art, and art wasn't supposed to look nice; it was supposed to make you feel something.' Rainbow Rowell, "Eleanor & Park"

Artists I love

Name:

Style:

Years active:

Movement:

Media:

Influences:

Comments:

'Do not draw before you paint – it will restrict your brush.' Toni Onley

Artists I love

Name:

Style:

Years active:

Movement:

Media:

Influences:

Comments:

Artists I love

Name:

Style:

Years active:

Movement:

Media:

Influences:

Comments:

'If you ask me what I came to do in this world, I, an artist, will answer you: I am here to live out loud.' Émile Zola

'Any fool can be happy. It takes a man with real heart to make beauty out of the stuff that makes us deep.' Clive Barker, "Days of Magic, Nights of War"

Artists I love

Name:

Style:

Years active:

Movement:

Media:

Influences:

Comments:

Artists I love

Name:

Style:

Years active:

Movement:

Media:

Influences:

Comments:

'Drawing, within the visual arts, seems to hold the position of being closest to pure thought.' John Elderfield

Artists I love

Name:

Style:

Years active:

Movement:

Media:

Influences:

Comments:

Artists I love

Name:

Style:

Years active:

Movement:

Media:

Influences:

Comments:

'My attitude towards drawing is not necessarily about drawing.

It's about making the best kind of image I can make, it's about talking as clearly as I can.' Jim Dine

Artists I love

Name:

Style:

Years active:

Movement:

Media:

Influences:

'A work of art which did not begin in emotion is not art.'
Paul Cézanne

Comments:

Artists I love

Name:

Style:

Years active:

Movement:

Media:

Influences:

Comments:

'lose your schematic conventions by finding some surprising symbol or shape in the welter of shades, and draw that.' Adam Gopnik

Artists I love

Name:

Style:

Years active:

Movement:

Media:

Influences:

Comments:

'Once I start making marks on the paper, it becomes more about responding to these marks and less about copying the image...' Mark Demsteader

Artists I love

Name:

Style:

Years active:

Movement:

Media:

Influences:

Comments:

'Drawing is the basis of art. A bad painter cannot draw. But one who draws well can always paint.' Arshile Gorky

Artists I love

Name:

Style:

Years active:

Movement:

Media:

Influences:

Comments:

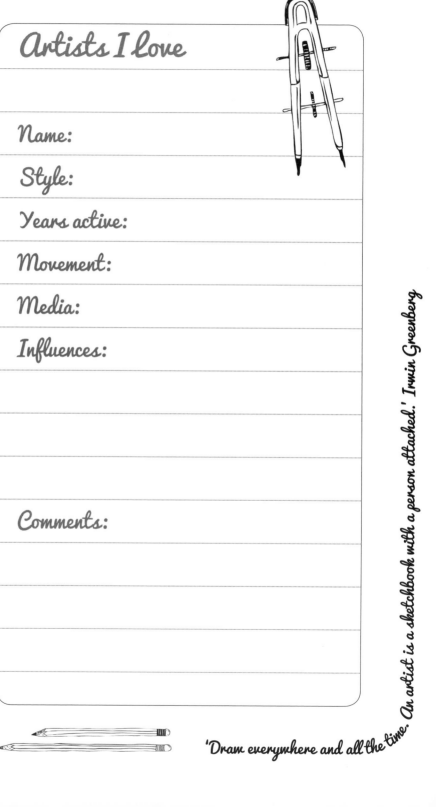

Artists I love

Name:

Style:

Years active:

Movement:

Media:

Influences:

Comments:

'Draw everywhere and all the time. An artist is a sketchbook with a person attached.' Irwin Greenberg

Artists I love

Name:

Style:

Years active:

Movement:

Media:

Influences:

Comments:

paint

Street Art I love

Where:

Artist? :

Style:

Medium:

Description/sketch:

'That way I can find out what I'm feeling, then use those ideas in my paintings and drawings.' Robert Levers

'I make sure to have time to draw everyday.

Street Art I love

Where:

Artist? :

Style:

Medium:

Description/sketch:

'Don't let the daily routine kill your creativity. Remember who you were before you got that job.' Morr Meroz, "Making an Animated Short"

MY SKETCHES & DOODLES : INSPIRATION

133

Street Art I love

Where:

Artist?:

Style:

Medium:

Description/sketch:

'Painting is the passage from the chaos of the emotions to the order of the possible.' Balthus

'I see my studio like a laboratory, where I work like an investigator – it's almost forensic. I love the discovery process in painting.' Ross Bleckner

Street Art I love

Where:

Artist?:

Style:

Medium:

Description/sketch:

'The first writing of the human being was drawing, not writing.' Marjane Satrapi

Street Art I love

Where:

Artist?:

Style:

Medium:

Description/sketch:

'Drawing is the "bones" of art. You have to be able to walk before you can run.' Dion Archibald

Street Art I love

Where:

Artist?:

Style:

Medium:

Description/sketch:

Street Art I love

Where:

Artist?:

Style:

Medium:

Description/sketch:

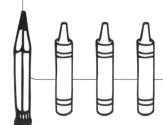

Street Art I love

Where:

Artist?:

Style:

Medium:

Description/sketch:

'It's hard to fake emotion behind the hand that draws. When eye and hand become friends, then drawing takes on a life of its own.' Gillian Redwood

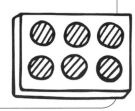

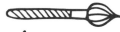

Street Art I love

Where:

Artist?:

Style:

Medium:

Description/sketch:

'I prefer drawing to talking.'

Street Art I love

Where:

Artist?:

Style:

Medium:

Description/sketch:

Street Art I love

Where:

Artist?:

Style:

Medium:

Description/sketch:

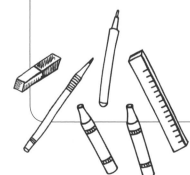

Street Art I love

Where:

Artist? :

Style:

Medium:

Description/sketch:

Everyday Inspiration

Note here places or things that inspire you,
such as a certain view or street, buildings,
found objects, the shadow cast through grating...

Name or description:

Where:

Comments:

My sketch:

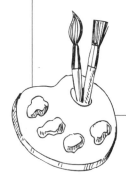

'The paintbrush is the key. The paintbrush is the door to another dimension.' Luhran

'The canvas is the door to another dimension.' Luhran

Everyday Inspiration

Name or description:

Where:

Comments:

My sketch:

'Drawing and colour are not separate at all; in so far as you paint, you draw. The more the colour harmonizes, the more exact the drawing becomes.' Paul Cézanne

Everyday Inspiration

Name or description:

Where:

Comments:

My sketch:

'Good drawing forms the "bones" on which a strong painting hangs.' Chris Bingle

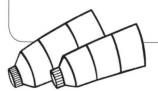

Everyday Inspiration

Name or description:

Where:

Comments:

My sketch:

Everyday Inspiration

Name or description:

Where:

Comments:

My sketch:

'When I look at a drawing of a person, I look at that person as living.' Francesco Clemente

Everyday Inspiration

Name or description:

Where:

Comments:

My sketch:

Art Calendar

Use this space to note down shows, exhibitions and publications to remember:

January:

February:

'Draw, Antonio,
draw draw and
don't waste time!'
Michelangelo

'Drawing not only develops hand-eye coordination, it teaches one to really observe, to see, as nothing else ever will.' Nancy Marculewicz

March:

April:

'Art is a collaboration between God and the artist, and the less the artist does the better.' Adré Gide

May:

June:

'Art will remain the most astonishing activity of mankind born out of struggle between wisdom and madness, between dream and reality in our mind.' Magdalena Abakanowicz

July:

August:

'As my artist's statement explains, my work is utterly incomprehensible and is therefore full of deep significance.' Bill Waterson, "Calvin and Hobbes"

September:

October:

'Let whoever may have attained to so much as to have the power of drawing know that he holds a great treasure.' Michelangelo

November:

December:

'Personality is everything in art and poetry.' Goethe

MY SKETCHES & DOODLES · ART CALENDAR

155

'The creation of a single world comes from a huge number of

My Sketches & Clippings

Here are some blank pages for your own sketches and doodles, or to stick/clip in articles, gallery ticket stubs, postcards or anything you like!

'I would rather die of passion than of boredom.' Vincent van Gogh

'I'm just interested in meditating on certain ideas, and I like to draw: that's my way of thinking.' Ben Nicholson

'Drawing is a way to keep subjects fresh.'
Jack Hambleton

Clippings

'Life is a winking light in the darkness.' Hayao Miyazaki

ART

My Sketches

'What I like about photographs is that they capture a moment that's gone forever, impossible to reproduce.' Karl Lagerfeld

'We don't make mistakes, just happy little accidents.' Bob Ross

'You might as well ask an artist to explain his art, or ask a poet to explain his poem. It defeats the purpose. The meaning is only clear thorough the search.' Rick Riordan

My Sketches

'Only put off until tomorrow what you are willing to die having left undone.' Pablo Picasso

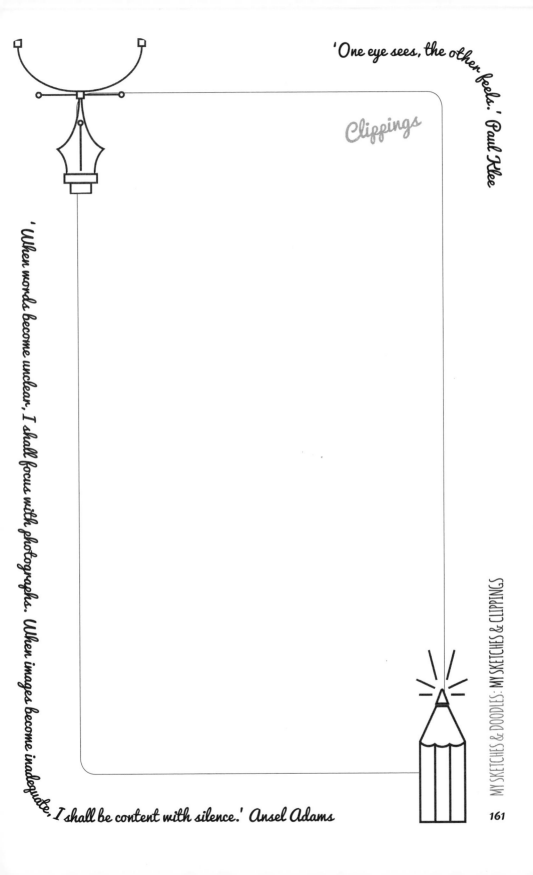

'One eye sees, the other feels.' Paul Klee

Clippings

'When words become unclear, I shall focus with photographs. When images become inadequate, I shall be content with silence.' Ansel Adams

My Sketches

'The painter has the Universe in his mind and hands.' Leonardo da Vinci

Clippings

'Art without emotion its like chocolate cake without sugar. It makes you gag.' Laurie Halse Anderson, "Speak"

My Sketches

'Every human is an artist. The dream of your life is to make beautiful art.' Miguel Ruiz, The Four Agreements: "A Practical Guide to Personal Freedom"

'Art should comfort the disturbed and disturb the comfortable.' Banksy

'Drawing is like making an expressive gesture with the advantage of permanence.' Henri Matisse

My Sketches

Clippings

'Drawing keeps the eye fresh, the mind alive, and intuition nimble.' Timothy Nero

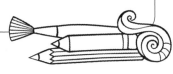

My Sketches

'Modern paintings are like women, you'll never enjoy them if you try to understand them.' Freddie Mercury

'A blank canvas...has unlimited possibilities.' Stephanie Perkins, "Isla and the Happily Ever After"

Clippings

'Drawing is the representation of form the graphic expression of a visual experience.' Walter J. Phillips

'Art is the child of nature in whom we trace the features of the mothers face.' Henry Wadsworth Longfellow

My Sketches

'It's a lot more difficult to perform one.' Chuck Palahniuk

'It's easy to attack and destroy an act of creation.

Clippings

'Art is the reason I get up in the morning, but the definition ends there. It doesn't seem fair that I'm living for something I can't even devine.' Ani DiFranco

My Sketches

'In the haunted house of life, art is the only stair that doesn't break.' Tom Robbins

Clippings

'Treat a work of art like a prince: let it speak to you first.' Arthur Schopenhauer

'All forms of madness, bizarre habits, awkwardness in society, general clumsiness, are justified in the person who creates good art.' " Roman Payne, Rooftop Soliloquy"

My Sketches

'I cannot rest, I must draw, however poor the result, and when I have a bad time come over me it is a stronger desire than ever.' Beatrix Potter

'Creativity is an act of defiance.' Twyla Tharp

Clippings

'We work in the dark – we do what we can – we give what we have. Our doubt is our passion, and our passion is our task. The rest is the madness of art.' Henry James, "The Middle Years"

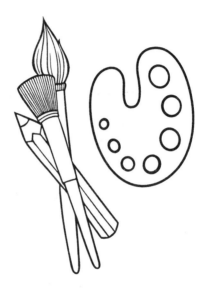

For further journals, notebooks, calendars
and illustrated books on a wide range of subjects,
in various formats, please look at our website:
www.flametreepublishing.com